MATT CHRISTOPHER

On the Ice with ...

Tara Lipinski

MATT CHRISTOPHER

On the Ice with...
Tara Lipinski

Little, Brown and Company
Boston   New York   London

First Edition

Library of Congress Cataloging-in-Publication Data

Christopher, Matt.
    On the ice with — Tara Lipinski / Matt Christopher. — 1st ed.
        p.   cm.
    Summary: Describes the life and skating career of the young woman who won a gold medal in figure skating at the 1998 Olympics.
    ISBN 0-316-14257-3
    1. Lipinski, Tara, 1982–   — Juvenile literature.   2. Skaters — United States — Biography — Juvenile literature.   [1. Lipinski, Tara, 1982–   .   2. Ice skaters.   3. Women — Biography.]   I. Title.
GV850.L56C57   1999
796.91'2'092 — dc21
[B]   98-36098

10 9 8 7 6 5 4 3 2 1

COM-MO

Printed in the United States of America

Contents

MATT CHRISTOPHER

On the Ice with...

Tara Lipinski

Chapter One:
1984-1986

An Olympic Moment

In the living room of the home of Pat and Jack Lipinski in Sewall, New Jersey, the television was on and tuned to the 1984 Olympic Games.

Two-year-old Tara, the Lipinskis' only child, idly played on the floor, while Pat, her mother, busied herself in the kitchen.

All of a sudden Pat Lipinski heard her daughter squeal with delight. Curious, she went into the living room to see what was making her daughter so happy.

On the television, three athletes stood on a podium, flowers in their arms and Olympic medals hanging from ribbons around their necks. In front of the television, wide-eyed little Tara stood on top of a plastic box, imitating the scene she saw on the television.

When she looked at her mother, she squealed again and said, "I want some flowers and a ribbon."

Pat smiled. Tara was an active, precocious child who had stood on her own when only six months old and had begun to walk by her first birthday. Nothing Tara did surprised her.

It was hard for her to refuse her daughter anything, and Pat happily responded to Tara's request. She gave her a small bunch of flowers and looped a strand of brightly colored ribbon around her neck.

On that day, Tara Lipinski began to dream about the Olympic Games.

And while neither the mother nor the daughter yet knew it, in only fourteen years, that scene would be repeated. When it was, it would not be the product of a child's imagination. It would be for real. An Olympic gold medal would hang around Tara's neck.

Pat, a secretary, and Jack, a young businessman who was attending law school, had married in 1980. Two years later, on June 10, 1982, Pat gave birth to a daughter. The Lipinskis decided to name her Tara after the name of the plantation in Pat's favorite movie, *Gone with the Wind*.

Jack had been an athlete when he was younger, playing soccer and lacrosse in school. Although many of his friends thought he would be disappointed with a daughter, Jack was pleased. Before the baby was born, he had worried that if he had a son, the child might feel pressured into playing sports, as he had sometimes felt while growing up. Jack thought it would be different for a girl. He was relieved when Tara was born. She could be anything she wanted to be, he thought.

Tara thrived on the attention she received as an only child. Her mother's cousin Phil and his wife, Edith, who Tara referred to as her aunt and uncle, lived nearby with their two young sons. Tara had lots of fun playing and trying to keep up with her two older cousins.

As a result, she seemed to mature faster than most children her age. Although she was small, she mastered physical skills, such as climbing out of her crib and riding a bike, earlier than other kids. She had so much energy that her mother was constantly on the lookout for activities to keep her daughter occupied.

When Tara was three, her mother saw an advertisement in the newspaper for a nearby roller-skating rink. The rink was giving away Care Bears, popular stuffed animals.

Pat knew that Tara loved stuffed animals and

thought a morning of roller-skating might tire her daughter out for the day. She loaded Tara into the car and drove over to the rink.

When Pat first tried to put the rented skates on Tara's tiny feet, Tara screamed and cried. She didn't like the feel or look of the skates. She wanted to go home.

But Pat pointed to the other children, who were wheeling around the rink and having fun. Several children were about Tara's age, and Pat told her daughter that if she wanted to play with them, she would have to wear the skates.

Tara looked around and stopped crying. Her mother took her hand and guided her carefully onto the surface of the rink.

At first, Tara couldn't stay upright. Every time she tried to move, her feet slid out from under her and she tumbled down. But she didn't cry. She just waited for her mother to lift her up. Then she would try to skate again.

Each time she did, Tara got a little better. Soon she was able to get back on her feet by herself, and after an hour or so, she rarely fell. She learned to take several short, quick running steps to build up momentum, then roll across the rink on her own, giggling and bumping into the other children.

When it was time to go, Pat took off Tara's skates and asked the rink attendant for Tara's Care Bear. But the attendant explained that Pat had misunderstood the ad. He said that in order to receive the stuffed animal, she would have to sign her daughter up for a minimum of ten lessons.

Pat saw the look of disappointment on Tara's face. Skating was fun, but she really wanted a Care Bear.

Pat didn't want Tara to get upset. Besides, she thought, Tara had enjoyed skating. Maybe skating lessons would provide a good outlet for her energy.

"Do you want to come here every week?" she asked.

"YES!" cried Tara. So her mother signed Tara up for ten weekly lessons, and Tara got her Care Bear. On the way home, Tara was all smiles as she held tight to her stuffed animal and jabbered excitedly about skating.

The Olympics were still far in the future, but Tara was on her way.

Chapter Two:
1986–1988

Rolling On

Pat half-expected her daughter to tire of skating. She really didn't even care if Tara took all ten lessons. She knew that it was hard for a three-year-old to stay focused on something like skating lessons.

But Tara surprised her. She enjoyed being at the rink, and she loved taking lessons with the other children. The instructors made the lessons fun. They played music and made up skating games. While the kids played, their skating skills slowly improved. Every time Tara and her mother returned home after skating, she could hardly wait to tell her father all about it.

Pat always sat in the stands with the other parents as their kids wheeled around the rink. Although she usually brought a book to read, more often than not she ended up just watching her daughter roller-skate and have fun. As far as she could tell, Tara was just another toddler trying not to fall.

At the end of the ten lessons, the children got to put on a Christmas show. They dressed up as reindeer and skated to Christmas carols.

Tara loved performing in front of the crowd. For weeks, it was all she could talk about.

The mother of one of Tara's skating friends learned that another roller rink had a special "Tiny Tot" skating program, specifically designed for younger children. She asked Pat if she'd like to sign their kids up for the program together. Pat quickly agreed.

After Tara's third group session at the new rink, one of the instructors approached Pat as she and Tara were preparing to leave.

Although Pat hadn't noticed, the instructor had quickly realized that Tara was something special. She was better coordinated than many of the other children and seemed to learn faster. The instructor told Pat that Tara had potential as a skater and suggested that in addition to her group lesson, Tara should take a private lesson once a week.

Pat was surprised, but she already knew how much Tara loved to skate. She thought about it for a moment, then asked Tara if she wanted to skate more each week.

"Yes!" was Tara's enthusiastic reply.

The more Tara skated, the more she loved it. Within a few weeks, she began taking two private lessons a week. A few months later, she began taking three a week and then four. Within a year, Tara was taking private lessons nearly every day of the week.

Although the extra instruction took a lot of time and money, Pat and Jack Lipinski didn't mind. They wanted their daughter to be happy and assumed that at some point Tara would tire of going to the rink every day.

Taking private lessons allowed Tara to improve quickly. She soon left other skaters her age far behind. In order to keep Tara motivated, her instructors, Charlie Kirchner and Kathy DeFelice, exposed her to a wide variety of skating styles. Although she was only four years old, they knew it would only be a matter of time before Tara started competing as a solo skater. Part of singles competition included school figures, precise patterns each skater must trace on the rink. Young children often become bored with the tedious repetition of school figures. But

Tara never got bored with skating. She loved being on skates and feeling in control of her movements.

They also had Tara practice pairs skating. In pairs, two skaters skate together to music, matching each other's movements. She even tried speed skating, rolling around the rink as quickly as she could. As Tara late wrote in her autobiography, *Triumph on Ice*, "I liked everything."

The only thing that stopped Tara from skating was roller hockey. Tara and her mother had to leave the rink each evening when teams of older children began arriving to play roller hockey, a game almost identical to ice hockey.

Tara didn't realize that few girls played roller hockey, particularly five year olds. All she knew was that if she played roller hockey, she'd be able to spend even more time at the rink.

First she bugged Charlie Kirchner, who ran the roller hockey program, for her own roller hockey stick, which players use to hit the roller hockey ball, similar to a hockey puck. He cut a regular stick down to Tara's size. Then Tara told her mother that she wanted to play roller hockey, too, so they asked Charlie Kirchner if she could play. He knew that

9

Tara was already one of the best skaters at the rink, so he agreed.

The first time Tara showed up at the rink, she was the only girl who had signed up to play. She was also the youngest player. Everyone else was at least eight years old. Most of the boys were at least twice her size.

The boys couldn't believe that a girl wanted to play roller hockey. Some of the boys, and a few parents, told Charlie Kirchner they didn't think a girl should be allowed to play.

Kirchner had expected that reaction. So he had a group of skaters, including Tara, line up on the rink. He told them that when he blew his whistle, he wanted everyone to skate backward to the wall.

For many children, just learning to skate forward is hard. Skating backward is an even more difficult skill to master, but one that the sport of roller hockey requires.

He blew the whistle, and everyone tried to skate backward. A few boys pushed off and moved slowly back, looking over their shoulders to keep from bumping into someone. But most of the boys hardly moved. They didn't have any idea how to skate backward. Most of those who tried fell after taking only one or two strides, their arms and legs splayed out awkwardly.

But one player didn't have a problem. When the whistle blew, Tara expertly skated backward to the wall, seemingly without effort.

The boys looked at her, amazed. Tara had learned how to skate backward months before. By now, she could do it without even thinking about it.

"All right," said Kirchner to the group, "does anyone have a problem playing with a girl now?"

No one said a word. The sport of roller hockey was added to Tara's skating résumé.

She loved playing. Despite her small size, her skating skills allowed her to become one of the best players in the league. In fact, her size was an advantage to her, since she was small enough to squeeze between defenders. She scored a lot of goals.

At the same time she was playing roller hockey, Tara began competing in roller-skating competitions. Roller-skating competitions are very similar to figure-skating competitions. Skaters demonstrate their various moves while skating to music.

Tara was already able to do much more than

roller-skate backward and forward. She could do basic jumps and spins, such as the axel, which is named after Axel Paulsen, the first skater to perfect the move. When doing an axel, a skater glides forward, leaps in the air off one foot, spins, then lands backward on the opposite foot.

Tara loved doing maneuvers like the axel, and she loved competing. She got to wear fancy skating dresses and travel all over the state to attend competitions far from her home. At age five, she won her first event, a regional competition. Tara was already one of the best skaters her age in her area. Soon she was traveling to competitions nearly every weekend.

She loved competing so much that she eventually quit roller hockey. She needed more time for singles practice, and she didn't like it when she got knocked down and someone skated over her fingers!

When Tara was six, Pat Lipinski's friend Janet suggested that Tara should try ice-skating. She told Pat that ice-skating provided better opportunities for a talented skater. Unlike roller-skating, ice-skating is an Olympic sport.

At first, Tara's mom dismissed her friend's suggestion. "Tara has fun roller-skating," she told her. "That's all that matters." Besides, she told Janet, the nearest ice-skating rink was miles away. She was already spending hours each week driving Tara to roller-skating rinks. She couldn't see adding more.

As far as Tara's parents were concerned, skating was just another activity that kept their daughter busy. They didn't expect her to grow up and become a skater, much less compete in the Olympic Games. She was just a young child.

But Pat's friend wouldn't stop talking about it. Finally, around Christmas 1988, Tara's mother relented. One day the Lipinskis took Tara to an ice-skating rink. As Pat Lipinski later remembered, she just wanted to prove to Janet that although Tara was a talented roller-skater, she would be a terrible ice-skater.

In less than an hour, Tara's mother would change her mind.

Chapter Three:
1988

Taking to the Ice

The sport of figure skating has a long history. People have been skating on ice for hundreds of years. Historians have learned that as far back as 1175, people in London, England, were skating over ice by strapping animal bones to their shoes and pushing themselves along with long sticks.

Several hundred years later, in the Netherlands, the first ice skates were made by attaching long iron blades to wooden shoes.

By the 1700s, the pastime had become so popular that people started to organize it formally. Skating clubs were formed, and in the mid-1800s, skating was established in the United States.

At first, people just skated for fun or to get from one place to another. In the Netherlands, for instance, people skated on the frozen canals to get from town to town. Even today, when the winters are cold enough that all the canals freeze, thousands of Dutch skaters compete in a big race between cities.

Then, in the 1860s, an American ballet dancer named Jackson Haines took up skating. He soon realized that it was possible to combine the two disciplines. While skating, he performed many of the dance moves he knew from ballet — including jumps and spins through the air.

People loved watching him skate, and he became famous, even touring Europe to demonstrate this new style of skating, which he called international skating. Soon, people who were not ballet dancers were imitating him.

Modern figure skating evolved from this style. By the late 1800s, so many people were figure skating that groups and clubs began to make rules for the sport and hold competitions. In 1908, figure skating became an Olympic sport.

But at first, competitive figure skating was a dull sport for spectators. Competitions focused on the marks the skater's blades made on the ice, not on how the skater moved over the surface. That's why the sport is called *figure* skating, because of the figures the skate blade makes as it cuts into the ice.

That all changed in 1928. At the Olympics that year, a fifteen-year-old Norwegian girl, Sonja Henie, changed the sport forever. Although she could trace figures as well as any skater in the world, she began doing leap and jumps and spins that no one had ever tried before. Moreover, she moved gracefully and wore fancy clothing that showed off her unique style and beauty.

Spectators and judges were thrilled with her performance. She won the gold medal, her first of three. From that day forward, figure skating has been a sport that seeks to balance athleticism with the artistry of dance.

When Tara Lipinski arrived at an ice-skating rink for the first time, neither she nor her parents knew much about figure skating. The Lipinskis rented a tiny pair of skates, laced them to their daughter's feet, and escorted her onto the ice.

At first, Tara held on to the boards that surrounded the ice surface and watched as other skaters whirled past. Then, with her parents looking on, she took a tentative step out onto the ice.

Wham! As soon as Tara let go of the boards, her feet slipped out from beneath her and she landed hard on her knees. But she wasn't hurt. She struggled to her feet and tried once more to skate.

Slam! This time she landed on her rear end. Tara was surprised. Roller-skating had always been easy. Ice-skating was hard!

Tara's father looked at his daughter fallen prone on the ice and whispered to his wife, "She'll never be an ice-skater." Tara's mother breathed a big sigh of relief. Although she didn't want Tara to fail, she also didn't want to have to drive for hours to find an ice rink for Tara's practices. The nearest rink that offered lessons was in Delaware, an hour away from their New Jersey home. As she watched her daughter fall, she assumed that Tara would soon tire of trying to ice-skate.

As her parents watched, Tara fell again and again. Finally, her mother walked over to the boards, where Tara was holding on after falling once more.

"How about some hot chocolate?" she asked brightly. She was sure Tara would jump at the opportunity to stop skating and drink some hot chocolate. Then they could all go home.

17

But Tara surprised her. She wasn't discouraged at all. "No," she said, "I want to skate."

Tara's mother shook her head in disbelief. Then she and her husband walked toward the snack bar to get some hot chocolate for themselves.

While they were gone, Tara kept trying to skate. Even though she had fallen every time she'd tried, she had already noticed the difference between roller-skating and ice-skating. As she watched the other skaters, she saw some leaping through the air and spinning around. She noticed that they went much faster than roller-skaters and were able to leap better. Compared to ice skates, roller skates were heavy.

But she did more than just watch. She observed the other skaters carefully. She noticed how they positioned their feet as they alternately skated and glided. She studied how they positioned their bodies over their skates and how they lightly transferred their weight from one foot to the other. Then she tried to skate again.

At first she kept falling. But she kept trying, and within a few minutes, she was able to take a few tentative strides.

With each step, her confidence grew. All of a sudden, she discovered that she was able to take what she had learned about roller-skating and make use of it on ice skates. In a few minutes she felt nearly as comfortable on the ice as she did at the roller rink.

Then she decided to try some of the moves she used on roller skates, like jumping and spinning and skating backward. She took a few strides to build up speed, then leaped into the air.

She landed hard and wobbled on her ankles for a moment, but stayed upright. She could do it!

Then she jumped into the air and spun around. Although she almost fell, she kept her balance, took a quick step, and glided on.

She felt as free on her ice skates as she did on her roller skates. She stopped worrying about falling and began concentrating on her moves. Each time she tried and succeeded, her confidence grew.

Soon Tara was almost alone on the ice, skating as if she had done so every day of her young life. The other skaters, who only a few moments before had laughed sympathetically as they saw her stumble and fall, now stood back, amazed. They had never seen anyone improve so quickly, and they had never seen a six-year-old do what Tara was doing her first time on the ice.

Tara's parents returned from the refreshment stand and saw everyone standing around and watching a lone child skate. Then they realized that that lone child was Tara!

Tara's dad looked at her mother and started to laugh. "Looks like you'll be driving to Delaware," he quipped.

All she could do was nod and smile.

Chapter Four:
1989–1993

A Skating Life

Overnight, Tara's already busy schedule got even busier. She still enjoyed roller-skating and didn't want to quit. She wanted to roller-skate *and* ice-skate. In addition to all that, she had started first grade.

In order to do everything she wanted, Tara embarked on a schedule that few adults could maintain, much less a young child. At first she practiced roller-skating three days a week and ice-skating three days a week. On Sundays, she practiced both!

Then she started working even harder and on many days practiced both sports. She would wake up in the morning before the sun rose, get dressed, and quickly eat breakfast. Then her mother would driver her to the roller-skating rink for lessons. Then Tara went to school all day. As soon as the final bell rang, she raced from her class to the parking lot, where her mother was waiting in the car. As her mother drove to the Delaware Ice Skating Development Center, Tara ate a snack and did her homework in the backseat. She was spending at least four hours every day on skates.

She continued to improve in each sport and even began participating in ice-skating competitions. In her first ever competition, she finished second.

But her main competitive focus remained on roller-skating. Nearly every weekend she was off to another big competition.

Although Tara quickly became a very good ice-skater, she was a great roller-skater. Over the next three years, she won more than fifty ribbons and trophies, culminating in winning a national junior competition when she was only nine years old.

The summer after Tara finished third grade, Jack Lipinski, who had finished law school and now worked for a corporation, got a new job. He was named vice president of a petroleum company.

It was a big promotion and meant that he would make a great deal of money. The Lipinskis needed the extra income, because Tara's lessons were costing a small fortune. But there was just one problem. The new job was in Texas.

That summer, Tara and her family packed up and moved from New Jersey to Sugar Land, a suburb of Houston. Tara hated leaving all her friends and relatives behind. Most of all, though, she hated leaving the Delaware ice-skating rink.

Although her parents quickly found both a roller rink and an ice-skating rink for Tara to practice at, Tara didn't adjust well to the move.

The normally happy young girl suddenly turned sullen and moody. She cried often and had fits of anger.

Her parents were worried about her. Although they hadn't ever pressured their daughter into skating, they were afraid that her hectic and often stressful schedule was becoming too much for her. It didn't help that the only ice-skating rink in Houston was at a shopping mall. In order to practice in private, Tara and her mother had to get up at three in the morning so Tara could take lessons before the mall opened! The Lipinskis wanted to make sure she lived a normal life like other children.

On top of everything else, all the private lessons

were becoming increasingly expensive. After hours of discussion, Tara's parents decided that she could no longer continue to participate in both roller-skating and ice-skating. They now realized that ice-skating offered Tara the most opportunity, so they told Tara she would have to stop taking roller-skating lessons.

The decision only increased Tara's unhappiness. She was just a little girl and didn't understand.

Her parents remained firm. They explained to her that now she would have time for other activities, and they tried to interest her in baton twirling, modeling, gymnastics, and dance. But Tara would attend a lesson or two, then demand to quit. She only wanted to skate.

Then, ever so slowly, Tara began to adjust to her new life. She made new friends. She got along well with her new ice-skating coach, Megan Faulkner. And that Christmas, her parents got her a horse, which she named Moonray. Soon she was taking riding lessons. She became such a good rider that she entered and won a few competitions.

But keeping a horse was expensive, and Tara's skating lessons became even more demanding and more costly. Her parents loved her, but something had to give.

They told Tara that she had to decide between Moonray and skating. They felt terrible asking their daughter to make such a difficult decision, but they had no choice.

To their surprise, Tara understood. She loved her horse, she told them, but skating was her life. She couldn't imagine not being able to skate.

Now that she was focusing solely on figure skating, Tara improved rapidly. There was less competition in Texas, and she dominated the local skating scene in her age group.

In the summer of 1992, just as she turned ten years old, Tara and her mother returned to New Jersey so Tara could attend a special camp at her old rink in Delaware. Tara loved being back at the rink and being close to her relatives again.

At the end of the summer, her coach, Jeff DiGregorio, had a long talk with Tara's mother. He explained to her that Tara was a special skater, someone who had the potential to become a world or Olympic champion. But in order to reach her full potential, he felt that she needed intensive one-on-one training. Although DiGregorio knew that Tara enjoyed training with Megan Faulkner, he felt that it would be best if Tara remained in Delaware to train. He even offered to find a host family willing to take Tara into their home when her mother returned to Texas.

Neither Tara nor her mother could bear the idea of having Tara stay with strangers. As much as they believed that DiGregorio was correct in his assessment of Tara's potential, they still had to return to Texas. After all, they were a family.

Back in Houston, Tara resumed her grueling training schedule, but now she began to struggle with the demands on her time. Both her schoolwork and her ice-skating started to suffer. By Christmas, she and her mother were both exhausted.

Tara and her parents realized how much better it would be for Tara if she were able to train back in Delaware. There, she wouldn't have to get up at three in the morning to train. The ideal situation would be for the family to move back near the rink.

But Jack Lipinski couldn't leave his job. The family needed his income, and he couldn't get a job on the East Coast to compare with his present position.

That winter and spring, Tara's parents spent hours talking, trying to decide what to do. They finally arrived at a difficult decision.

They decided that Tara and her mother would move to Delaware and get an apartment near the rink. Jack, meanwhile, would stay in Texas. Since training took so much time away from school, they decided to move the school to Tara. From now on, she would have private tutors.

All that would be expensive. In order to pay for the move, the Lipinskis refinanced their house and borrowed extra money from a bank.

Jack and Pat were making a huge sacrifice for their daughter, one that they knew was risky. It would be hard on the entire family to live apart, but they decided it was worth it. Tara loved to skate, and they wanted her to have every chance to reach her full potential.

As soon as the school year was over, just after Tara's eleventh birthday, she and her mother moved into a small apartment near the Delaware rink. Although they all talked together on the phone every evening and Tara's father visited every four or five weeks, it was still a difficult adjustment.

The only part that wasn't difficult for Tara was the skating. She loved being back at the rink. Under DiGregorio's direction, her training schedule increased dramatically.

Tara now skated for five forty-minute sessions each day. In addition to that, she did weight training to build strength and took ballet to help her move more gracefully on the ice. After all that, she still had to spend three or four hours each day with tutors and then do homework.

It was hard, but in many ways her new routine was easier than her old schedule in Texas. Tara loved being able to sleep until almost eight o'clock each morning. Then it was off to the rink for practice, which usually ended around noon. Then she ate lunch, lifted weights, took ballet, and met with her tutors. She was usually finished by six o'clock.

Although she missed seeing kids at school, she made up for it by making friends at the rink. The other skaters became an extended family to her, and she turned to them for support.

She would need it, for at age eleven, Tara Lipinski was more determined than ever to make her mark in figure skating.

Chapter Five:
1993

Ready to Compete

Under Jeff DiGregorio's guidance, Tara's training began to pay off. She now focused completely on singles skating, in which a skater performs on the ice alone. Although she was just a child, she was already skilled enough to learn the same jumps and other maneuvers executed by the greatest skaters in the world.

In the 1990s, women's figure skating has evolved into a sport that is incredibly demanding both athletically and artistically. In 1990, the International Skating Union (the governing body that runs the sport) phased out the compulsories, or school figures competition. The focus of competition was now solely on so-called free skating, in which the skater skates to music.

The change made a dramatic impact on the sport.

Since skaters no longer had to spend hours practicing the compulsories, they could spend more time practicing jumps and spins. In only a few years, the skill level of most skaters has increased dramatically. Where double jumps had once been standard, most world-class skaters are now expected to make triple jumps. At the same time, skaters are expected to perform the more difficult jumps smoothly and gracefully, making them look effortless.

Competitive figure skating is divided into two events: the short program and the free skate, or long program. In the short program, a skater has to perform eight required elements, or moves, set to music over two minutes and forty seconds. In the long program, a skater performs elements of his or her own choice set to music over a four-minute period.

Both programs are judged by experienced officials. The short program makes up one-third of a skater's final score, and the long program counts for the remaining two-thirds.

The judging process is complicated. As the skater performs, the judges watch closely. They often have had the opportunity to observe the skaters practice before the actual competition, so they know what to expect.

After each performance, the judges give the skater two scores, ranging from zero to six. The judges are allowed to score in the tenths of a point, such as 5.6, to make the scoring more precise.

The first score measures how well the individual elements are executed, taking into account their degree of difficulty. The second score reflects the artistic impression made by the entire performance, including the skater's speed, use of the rink, level of risk, height of jumps, spacing between elements, variety of elements used, and overall presentation.

After each program, the scores for each skater are compared to those of the other competitors. Skater are then ranked according to their combined score. The skater with the highest score wins the competition.

Scoring is done the same way at every level of competition. Skaters are grouped according to age and ability, ranging from the novice division, for young, beginning skaters, to the junior division, for those with more experience, all the way up to the senior division, for those skaters who have mastered elements required in the novice and junior categories.

The sport is organized on a regional, national, and world basis. Skaters generally begin competing in each category regionally, then, if they perform well enough, move on to national and world competitions.

As a result, skaters have to do a great deal of traveling. Not only do they have to learn to skate well; they also have to learn to do so under a variety of conditions.

Competition is intense. For although skating competitions affiliated with the International Skating Union are amateur competitions, national organizations such as the United States Figure Skating Association are allowed to offer some support to their most talented members. And once a skater qualifies for the senior level of competition, some events include cash awards. The best skaters, like those who make it to the Olympics, can become famous and earn thousands of dollars from endorsements. Skaters can then become wealthy by performing in ice shows and in professional skating competitions for television.

But for every young skater who makes it to the Olympics, thousands try and fail. Talent isn't enough to ensure success. Skaters have to remain motivated. At the highest levels, a skater must be one hundred percent committed to skating.

When Tara Lipinski returned to Delaware with her mother, she made that kind of commitment. By deciding to train full-time and leave school, she gave up the opportunity to live a normal life like other kids her age for the chance to become one of the best skaters in the world. She knew the odds were against her, but as Tara told everyone she met, "Skating is my life." She and her parents were determined to do everything they could to give her the opportunity to succeed.

Like most skaters, Tara had begun competing in the novice division. But by the time she moved back to Delaware, she had progressed so rapidly that she was ready to prepare to move up to junior competitions. Her coach was determined to provide her with the proper instruction she needed to compete at this higher level.

Tara was unique among skaters because she had started while so young. She generally found herself competing against skaters several years older.

Many skaters would have found it difficult to compete against older skaters. They would have been intimidated.

But not Tara! Perhaps because she was too young to know better, when she stepped onto the ice, she never thought about her age. In fact, her age and diminutive size actually worked to her advantage. Because she was usually the youngest skater competing, judges immediately knew who she was and paid attention to her. And although she was small — barely four-foot-six and about seventy pounds — she was incredibly strong for her size, which made it easier for her to complete jumps and other complicated elements.

By the time she returned to Delaware, Tara had already mastered the basic moves of the sport: jumps such as the axel, the lutz, the salchow, and toe loop, and other maneuvers such as the sit-spin, the spiral, and the camel.

But in order to continue moving up in her sport, she still needed to improve. Thus far, she had been able to get by doing doubles — jumps in which she would spin around twice in the air. Now she had to add triples to her program.

She also had to improve her artistic presentation. That's the only part of skating where her age and size worked against her. Because she was so young and so small, she simply didn't look as fluid and graceful as older skaters.

In the summer of 1993, Jeff DiGregorio set out to help Tara make it to the next level of skating.

She had never worked harder or longer or had so much fun before. She worked particularly hard on a triple jump called the triple toe loop.

The triple toe loop begins with the skater gliding backward. Then the skater pushes off on the outside edge of her skating foot and jumps into the air. While in flight, the skater must spin all the way around three times, then land on the outside edge of the same foot she took off on.

It is a very difficult element, because it all must be done while the skater is moving almost at top speed across the ice. It requires speed, strength, and incredible coordination.

Nearly every day, Tara spent hours working on the

triple toe loop. When she first tried it, she fell every single time. To Tara, it just didn't feel as though she had enough time in the air to spin three times before landing.

Yet she improved a little every day, jumping a little higher and spinning a little faster. In midsummer she began landing the jump. Once she did, she began to do so regularly. Tara discovered that performing triple toe loops was like riding a bike. If you've never done it before, it seems incredibly hard. But once you succeed, it starts to seem incredibly easy. A lot of skills required in sports are like that.

But Tara knew that the ability to land a triple toe loop wouldn't be enough to guarantee a win in competition. She wasn't the only skater who could land triples. She had to work equally hard on her artistic impression.

Taking ballet lessons helped. She became more flexible and more aware of her body. She and her coach also made sure that her costumes fit correctly and made her look more mature. And they were cautious about the music they selected for her to skate to. It had to be just right, neither too fast nor too slow, and with enough variety to make each jump and spin appear as if it was set to the music.

Late that summer, they began to create a short and long program to use in competition. Soon Tara would get her chance to win flowers and ribbons.

Chapter Six:
1994

Skating Around the World

Early in 1994, Tara, her parents, and her coaches decided that she was ready to begin competing. Since she was only eleven years old, they all knew it would probably be several years until she was able to compete in the senior division. Tara still had so far to go that neither she nor her parents nor her coach were giving the 1998 Olympic Games a serious thought. The Olympics of 2002 were a far more realistic goal.

Tara's first two competitions were the midwestern and the southwestern regional novice competitions. She won them both!

But neither Coach DiGregorio nor her parents allowed Tara to get overconfident. They reminded her that the other skaters at the regionals hadn't been the best. It would be very different at her next competition, the Novice Nationals. In only her third major skating competition, Tara would have to skate against the best young skaters in the country.

In late January, she traveled with her mother and her coach to Detroit, the site of the United States Figure Skating Association's National Championships. Dozens of skaters from all over the country would compete for the national titles in singles and pairs skating, in novice, junior, and senior divisions. Not only would Tara have the chance to compete, but she would also get to see some of the best skaters in the world.

Tara loved the competition. When she took to the ice, she leaped and jumped through the air with a speed and agility that the judges found astonishing. She even nailed her triple toe loop, a jump that many senior skaters were still struggling to perfect. Although she finished second, skaters from all over the country couldn't stop talking about the little girl who jumped so well. Tara and her coach were pleased.

Over the Fourth of July weekend, a big skating competition was taking placed in St. Louis, Missouri, as part of the United States Olympic Festival.

The Olympic-style competition was designed to prepare young athletes for international competition. An athlete had to be invited to compete.

Tara's surprisingly high finish in the Nationals had raised her profile in American figure skating. She desperately wanted to attend the Olympic Festival but hadn't been invited. Most of the skaters asked to compete were junior skaters, several years older than Tara and far more experienced.

But two weeks before the festival, Tara received a phone call. Another skater, Michele Cho, had been forced to drop out with an injury. Tara had been selected to appear in her place!

Tara was thrilled. But her mother and coach cautioned her not to get too excited or set her expectations too high. After all, she would have to compete against skaters who were much older and more experienced than she was. They didn't want her to be disappointed if she didn't do well.

Yet at the same time, they were cautiously optimistic. Just a week before, Tara had mastered yet another triple jump, the triple loop. It is nearly identical to the triple toe loop, except the jump has to begin with the skate blade fully on the ice. In the triple toe loop, a skater is allowed to dig the toe of the skate into the ice to help push off. The triple loop is far more demanding.

Tara loved attending the Olympic Festival. She got to stay in a dormitory with other athletes and meet people from all over the country. She had a lot of fun.

But when it came time to compete, Tara didn't forget why she was there. Fun was for later — now she had to concentrate on skating.

In a teal-colored dress with gold trim, Tara glided confidently over the ice surface to get loose, then paused and took a deep breath. She looked around. The arena was filled to capacity with thousands of skating fans. She had never skated before so many people in her life. When the music began to play, she started her short program.

It was an ambitious, exciting program designed to highlight her spectacular jumping ability. It even included a combination triple loop–double loop, in which a skater goes directly from one leap into another without pause. Combinations are very difficult.

When Tara took off at the beginning of a triple–

double combination, she was just another young skater with potential, not all that different from dozens of other young women all around the country. By the time she landed, all that had changed.

After twirling in the air like a top, Tara appeared to barely touch the ice before she was in the air again, completing the double loop portion of the combo. Then she gracefully glided over the ice, moving onto the next element without hesitation. As she did, the crowd cheered so loudly that Tara could hear their voices above the music.

The difficult combination had at once both surprised and pleased the crowd. Few people expected to see such a jump attempted by a novice skater, much less completed perfectly. For the rest of the program, the crowd cheered her every move.

Tara was ecstatic. She had never skated so well or had so much fun. Her performance was acknowledged by the judges, and at the end of the short program, Tara was in first place.

Now she began to realize what was at stake. If she won the competition, she would automatically be named a member of the United States junior world team and qualify for the 1994 World Junior Championships, to be held that fall in Hungary.

She barely had time to get nervous. The next day, she had to skate her long program.

Before she took to the ice, Coach DiGregorio told her about a dream he had had the previous night. "I dreamed you skated a clean program and got a standing ovation when it was over," he said.

Tara grinned. She knew her coach was just trying to give her confidence.

A few hours later, she was on the ice, skating to music from the opera *Samson and Delilah.* The program went by in a blur as Tara moved effortlessly between elements, nailing a total of three triple combinations and two double axel combinations.

When the music stopped, Tara took her bows. The crowd began to cheer, then, just as Coach DiGregorio had dreamed, they stood on their feet and gave her a standing ovation.

Tara was stunned. She waved to the crowd and grinned widely as she was showered with flowers tossed onto the ice from the stands.

A few moments later, the judges made official

what everyone in the crowd already knew. Tara Lipinski was the Olympic Festival's gold medalist!

In addition to the gold medal, the victory also earned Tara a five-thousand-dollar cash prize, money that her parents appreciated receiving. Including plane tickets, hotel rooms, and Tara's costume, it had cost nearly that much just for Tara to make it to the festival. For the year, they eventually spent nearly sixty thousand dollars to support Tara's career.

After the victory, Tara was surprised to learn that she was the youngest athlete ever to win a gold medal at the festival. She also received the Mary Lou Retton Award, named after the champion gymnast and given to the festival's outstanding female athlete. All of a sudden, Tara Lipinski was big news.

At a press conference, reporters crowded around her and peppered her with questions. Tara was a little overwhelmed. For most of the conference, she sat on an older skater's lap. All Tara could say was "I just wanted to do the best I could." But when a reporter asked her about competing in the 1998 Olympics, Tara admitted "My biggest dream is to win at the Olympics." Newspapers all over the country carried reports of her victory.

When she returned to Houston later that year, she discovered that she had become a celebrity. She received a key to the city, and in the fall she was the subject of a long profile in the *New York Times.*

The *Times* story brought Tara to the attention of the national media and identified her as someone to keep an eye on. Before the year was out, she had appeared on several television programs, including *Good Morning America.*

Yet while Tara's bubbly personality and obvious talent charmed most observers, others were more cynical. Some thought she was spoiled, while others questioned whether she had been pushed into competition by her parents. Although Tara and her mother both made it clear she skated only because she wanted to, similar questions would hound her over the next several years.

Before the World Championships, Tara proved that her victory at the Olympic Festival had been no fluke. First she had to take a test to qualify to compete as a junior. She passed it easily. Then she was invited to Germany to compete in the Blue Swords Cup. She finished first again. Tara particularly enjoyed the fact that, as at the Olympic Festival, she was allowed to stay in a dormitory with the other athletes. She liked making new friends, and staying by herself made her feel grown up.

The 1994 World Junior Championships were held over Thanksgiving weekend in Budapest, Hungary. In her first major international competition, Tara didn't expect to do very well. She just hoped to gain experience. After all, she was still the youngest skater at the competition.

She shocked the world by finishing fourth, narrowly missing a bronze medal. Moreover, she impressed her teammates and the team officials with her maturity and focus. Although she was the youngest person on the team, she had performed like a veteran.

In the stands after her performance, her father turned to her mother and said, "She's fourth in the world. Do you know how good that is?"

Pat Lipinski just nodded. "I know," she said. "I know."

In a few short years, the rest of the world would find out just how good Tara Lipinski was, too.

Chapter Seven:
1995–1996

The Nationals

After her impressive finish at the Worlds, Tara was heavily favored to win the National Junior Championships, to be held in Providence, Rhode Island, in February 1995. Before the competition, she worked extra hard and added yet another triple to her repertoire, a jump called the triple flip.

Yet for the first time in her life, Tara began to feel the pressure that often comes with the expectation of success. The press and officials of the USFSA began to speculate about Tara's future. Already they were beginning to compare her with American skaters such as Peggy Fleming and Dorothy Hamill, both of whom won Olympic gold medals. All this for a skater who had yet to win a national championship or even turn thirteen years old!

Unfortunately, in the blind draw held before

competition, Tara was selected to be the first skater to perform the short program. That's usually a disadvantage, because judges rarely give the first skater very high marks. They always leave enough room so that a skater can still score well enough to win.

Tara took to the ice in a sharp black velvet dress with matching black gloves. The outfit was striking but perhaps a little mature-looking for a skater Tara's age. She performed well, even completing the triple loop–double loop combination. She was smiling as she left the ice for the "kiss-and-cry" area, where skaters wait for their marks. It's called the kiss-and-cry area because if a skater performs well, she usually receives kisses and hugs from her supporters. But if a skater performs poorly, she is often left sobbing with disappointment.

Tara's technical marks were superb, but her artistic marks were disappointing. It seemed that some judges were put off by a twelve-year-old skater, particularly one in a black velvet dress. Fifteen-year-old Sydne Vogel of Alaska finished the short program in first place.

But at the beginning of the long program, Tara

was still within striking distance of Vogel. This time the draw went perfectly. She was scheduled to compete last, just after Vogel.

Vogel began her program strongly, then fell on one jump and stumbled on two others. She received high marks nevertheless, particularly for artistic presentation, and retained her hold on first place. But Tara still had to skate. She felt she had a good chance to win.

She skated boldly and confidently, nailing every element, including the brand-new triple flip.

When she left the ice to a standing ovation, she was certain she had won.

But when the scores were announced, the crowd began to boo and tears formed in Tara's eyes. Although her technical marks had been good enough to win, her artistic marks were poor, mostly 5.0's and 5.1's. She finished second to Vogel. The judges simply weren't prepared to make the twelve-year-old the national champion.

But Tara didn't cry for long. By the time she met the press, her tears had turned into determination. "I'll beat her next year," she announced.

DiGregorio concurred. "I would have put her first," he said. "She was the best in my eyes. I think there's still a national championship in her future."

Although Tara was pleased with the way she had skated, she was still disappointed with her finish. She looked forward to the 1995 World Junior Championships, scheduled to be held in March in Australia.

Tara spent two full weeks in Australia. She loved international competitions, particularly the camaraderie felt with other skaters.

She performed well but once again seemed to be penalized due to her age and diminutive stature. She placed fourth. When she returned to the United States and resumed her training in Delaware, she wondered if it was time to make some changes.

Although she enjoyed working with Coach DiGregorio, the Delaware rink was increasingly crowded. Finding enough time on the ice was difficult. She often had to practice her routines while dodging other skaters of lesser ability.

Tara and her mother also felt that her overall progress as a skater had slowed. Although she had now qualified to compete as a senior skater, Tara's improvement wasn't being acknowledged by the judges. Late in 1995, with the 1996 Senior Nationals on the horizon, Tara's first as a senior skater, Tara and Pat decided that it was time for Tara to find a new coach.

At the highest level of skating, the selection of a coach can make the difference between winning and losing. The best coaches work with only a handful of skaters. Tara's vast potential made her an attractive student for a coach to take. But she had to be careful in her selection. She didn't want to have to compete for her coach's time.

Tara and her mother crisscrossed the country, interviewing coaches and assessing their skating facilities.

They were particularly interested in two coaches. Frank Carroll had a reputation as one of the best coaches in the world. But he was focused on the training of Michelle Kwan, considered by many to be the best female skater in the world.

Richard Callaghan was in a similar position. He also had an international reputation. But he already had two world-class skaters under his tutelage, men's singles champion Todd Eldredge, and Nicole Bobek, the reigning national senior champion.

Just before Christmas, Tara returned to Texas for the holidays and began working out at the shopping mall again with her old Texas coach, Megan Faulkner. As they arrived at the rink one day, Faulkner raced out to meet her.

"Richard Callaghan has an opening!" she cried. Faulkner had just learned that Nicole Bobek had decided to change coaches.

Tara and her mother hopped back on a plane and flew to Detroit, where Callaghan coached at the Detroit Skating Club.

Callaghan was already familiar with Tara. He had been at many of her competitions with his own skaters and was impressed by what he had seen. He believed that Tara was already one of the best jumpers in skating. As she matured, he thought she had a chance to become the best skater in the world.

Tara spent several days in Detroit, working with Callaghan on a trial basis. Although she had grown accustomed to training her own way, Coach Callaghan's suggestions made sense. Even though he was strict, Tara seemed to thrive under his tutelage.

His other students, including Todd Eldredge, also made her feel right at home. Callaghan's skaters were all close to one another, and they made Tara feel like she was part of a family. When it was time to return to Texas, Tara told her mother she wanted to continue to work with Callaghan.

Her mother agreed, even though it would mean moving from their apartment in Delaware to Detroit and that they would still be separated from Tara's father.

Tara had precious little time to waste. The Senior Nationals were only a few weeks away, and before that she planned to compete in the 1996 World Junior Championships. For the next several months, she had to concentrate on competitions. All Callaghan could do was help her fine-tune the programs she had already developed under DiGregorio. There was no time to make any major changes.

Perhaps distracted by the coaching change, and looking ahead to the Senior Nationals, Tara was a disappointment at the junior championships. She finished fifth, behind several skaters whom she had routinely beaten in the past. But she was convinced that she was on the right track and looked forward to doing her best in the seniors competition.

The 1996 Senior Nationals were held in San Jose, California, in late January. Tara was the youngest skater on the roster.

Most experts expected fourteen-year-old Michelle Kwan, Tonia Kwiatkowski, and seventeen-year-old Nicole Bobek to compete for a medal. To most observers, Tara Lipinski was an afterthought. No one expected her to do very well in her first Senior Nationals.

Tara was nervous when she took to the ice for her short program. She couldn't believe she was skating against famous skaters like Kwan and Bobek. They were her heroes.

Instead of trying to win, Callaghan told her she should just concentrate on skating well. Where she would finish was out of her control. All she could do was skate her best.

She tried to stay focused. Although she made a few small mistakes, she still performed well enough to finish fifth in the short program.

Grace and serenity mingle in Tara Lipinski's countenance as she skates her free program at the World Figure Skating Championships in Switzerland in March 1997.

Tara's brilliant smile lights up the rink as she reaches the end of her free program at the 1997 World Championships.

AP/Wide World Photos

The top two skaters in the world—Michelle Kwan, silver medalist, and Tara Lipinski, gold medalist—at the 1997 World Championships.

With elegance and enthusiasm, Tara skates her free program at the White Ring in Nagano, Japan, during the 1998 Winter Olympics.

Tara's happiness is unrestrained after finishing a difficult and near-perfect routine in Nagano.

The three Olympic champions: Michelle Kwan, U.S.A., silver medalist;
Tara Lipinski, U.S.A., gold medalist; Lu Chen, China, bronze medalist.

Tara honors her country during the medal ceremony in Nagano.

Tara kisses her gold medal—it's a dream come true for the fifteen-year-old.

With her parents at her side, the youngest-ever women's figure skating Olympic gold medalist returns home triumphant.

A celebrity off the ice as well as on it, Tara takes the stage as a presenter in the fortieth annual Grammy Awards.

AP/Wide World Photos

Tara Lipinski's Record

Year	Competition	Placed
1994	Southwestern Novice Regionals	First
1994	Midwestern Novice Regionals	First
1994	National Novice Championships	Second
1994	U.S. Olympic Festival	First
1994	Blue Swords Cup	First
1995	World Junior Championships	Fourth
1995	National Junior Championships	Second
1995	World Junior Championships	Fourth
1996	World Junior Championships	Fifth
1996	National Senior Championships	Third
1996	World Senior Championships	Fifteenth
1996	Skate Canada	Second

(continued on next page)

Tara Lipinski's Record (cont.)

Year	Competition	Placed
1996	Trophée Lalique	Third
1996	Nations Cup	Second
1997	National Senior Championships	First
1997	Champions Series Final	First
1997	World Senior Championships	First
1997	Skate America	Second
1997	Trophée Lalique	Second
1998	National Senior Championships	Second
1998	Olympics	First

Her surprisingly good finish took all the pressure off. She had held her own with the top skaters in the country.

Nicole Bobek, who had finished third in the short program, was then forced to withdraw due to an injury. That opened the door for Tara to move up in the long program.

Skating with breezy self-confidence, she nailed her free skate, landing five triple jumps and a spectacular triple lutz–double toe combination. Although it wasn't enough to catch either Kwan or Kwiatkowski, each of whom skated almost perfectly, Tara vaulted into third place.

At the medal ceremony, Tara was in awe. She couldn't believe she was standing on the same podium with two skaters she admired so much. As she told a reporter later, "When I was standing on the podium, it was like 'Oh, my gosh, I've watched them on TV!'"

She didn't realize it yet, but there were already young skaters watching her on TV who felt the same way.

Chapter Eight:
1996

Ready for the World

Usually, the top three skaters at the Nationals qualify for the World Senior Championships. But when a skater is injured, they have the right to appeal for a position. Nicole Bobek, who had won a bronze medal at the 1995 Worlds, filed an appeal. U.S. skating officials had to decide whether to send Tara or Bobek to the competition.

When the decision was announced, Tara was delighted to learn that she had been selected. The officials apparently were worried that Bobek might not be recovered from her injury.

But their decision was also controversial, and they were criticized for bumping Bobek. Tara tried to avoid the debate, saying, "I'm friends with Nicole, so either way is okay with me."

Her training went well in the weeks before the

event, which was to be held in Edmonton, Alberta, in March. She arrived in Edmonton full of confidence. Although she didn't expect to win, she did hope to skate well.

The Worlds differ from most competitions in that there is a qualifying round in which each skater must compete. The top thirty make it to the finals. In her qualifying group, Tara finished a surprising second to Japanese star Midori Ito, easily qualifying for the finals.

Then Tara made a critical mistake. When it was time to perform her short program, instead of keeping to herself and staying focused, she watched Ito, one of her idols, skate.

But Ito was ill and had a rare off day, even falling on a jump. At a competition like the Worlds, a fall is enough to knock a skater out of medal competition.

As Tara heard Ito's marks being announced, it suddenly struck her that she had a chance to win. Instead of just concentrating on skating well, all of a sudden she was thinking about her scores and where she would finish.

When she took to the ice, she was distracted. From her first stride, she felt uncomfortable and out of sync. Early in her program, she attempted a double loop, an easy jump for her that she had successfully completed thousands of times.

But this time something went wrong. She was late on her takeoff, and her speed was off. After spinning around twice in the air, she landed awkwardly.

Thump! She fell hard and slid across the ice. Stunned, she scrambled to her feet and tried to complete her program.

To make up for her mistake, she decided to add a triple loop later in the program.

But she was still out of sync and fell for a second time. Although she finished her program without further incident, as she left the ice, she knew her performance had been terrible.

The judges confirmed her fears. Her marks were low. After the short program, she was in twenty-third place.

The controversy over her selection to compete in the Worlds returned. Critics both in and out of skating cited her disappointing short program as evidence that Tara wasn't ready for world-class competition.

But Tara was determined to prove her critics

wrong. The next day, she had a long talk with her coach, discussing the reasons she had failed. Callaghan pointed out that he thought it was a mistake to pay any attention to her competitors, as she had done by watching Ito. Her focus, he reiterated, should be only on her own performance, on skating well.

Since she was out of the running for a medal, Tara was an afterthought when the free skating program began. Defending world champion Lu Chen of China was in first place, with a narrow lead over Michelle Kwan.

Both Lu and Kwan were magnificent, but Kwan's program was slightly more daring, and she wrested first place from her Chinese rival.

By the time Tara took to the ice, Kwan was assured of the gold medal. No one expected Tara to skate well after her dismal performance in the short program.

But her mind was set on proving that she belonged on the world stage. As the music to the movie *Speed* blared over the loudspeakers and Tara began to skate, she blocked every thought from her head apart from the task at hand.

She nailed her first triple cleanly, and the crowd began to cheer. They knew how poorly she had skated in the short program, and most fans wanted her to succeed. She skated on and successfully completed another six triples during her program.

She finished eleventh in the free skate, which was good enough to move her into fifteenth place overall. It wasn't great, but compared to where she had started the free skate, she was pleased. She knew that if she had skated a clean short program, she could have easily finished in the top ten.

Now that her competition was over, she became a fan for the remainder of the Worlds. She was particularly pleased when her friend and teammate Todd Eldredge won the men's singles championship.

After the Worlds, Coach Callaghan told Tara that she needed to make some changes. She needed to develop new programs, and Callaghan wanted her to change her training routine as well. Tara was still growing, and he felt that she was placing too much emphasis on her jumps, trying each one over and over until it was perfect. He felt this was too hard on her body and inadvertently prevented her from focusing on the more subtle aspects of skating, such as her presentation.

Callaghan sensed correctly that Tara had to appear more sophisticated on the ice, so judges would stop thinking about her as a young girl. But at the same time he knew they had to be careful. If Tara tried to appear older than she was, she wouldn't be believable. He wanted her appearance to enhance her program, not detract from it.

He thought Tara had plenty of time. He dismissed any suggestion that she would be ready to compete in the 1998 Olympics, which were just two years away. Michelle Kwan, two years older than Tara and far more experienced, seemed like a shoo-in for a gold medal in 1998. She was skating well and winning every competition in sight. Tara would be just fifteen in 1998, and Callaghan didn't expect her to be ready. He focused on her continuing development and told Tara that it was far more realistic to think about competing in the 2002 Olympics.

With the pressure off, Tara and her coach started from scratch, working on Tara's hair, makeup, clothing, and music.

To help with the choreography of her routines, he enlisted Sandra Bezic, a world-renowned skating choreographer. At Bezic's suggestion, they selected music from the movies *Little Women* for the short program and *Sense and Sensibility* for the free skate. Megan Faulkner also agreed to serve as Tara's assistant coach, working with her every time she returned to Texas for a visit.

Tara also resumed work in ballet, training with a teacher named Marina Sheffer. Lessons with Callaghan focused on the nuances of skating, getting each element to flow together and making sure Tara never appeared awkward. He had her stop weight training, preferring that she build her strength by skating.

Tara enjoyed the opportunity to start fresh. Over the past year, it seemed as if all she had done was race from one competition to another. Although she was working hard, she enjoyed staying in one place for a while and began to get comfortable in her new home in Detroit.

For the first time in months, she was able to stick to a routine. After waking in the morning and grabbing a quick breakfast, Tara was on the ice every day at 8:30 A.M., warming up with Callaghan's other skaters.

Then Callaghan would put her through two rigorous practices, focusing first on her long program and then on her short program. After lunch she went back on the ice with Callaghan, working on specific moves.

Callaghan added a twist to her combinations. Instead of pairing a triple jump with a double, Callaghan inserted a triple salchow–triple loop combination. Very few skaters in the world, male or female, could perform a triple-triple combo. He knew that if Tara could do the move in competition, the judges would have to give her high marks.

Ever so slowly, she took what she learned and put it all together in her new programs. Soon she was ready to start competing again.

Her first competition was Skate Canada 1996, held that fall. With her new programs, Tara finished second. She even nailed the triple-triple!

A week later, she traveled to France to compete in the Trophée Lalique. As expected, Michelle Kwan won the event, but Tara finished third in an impressive field, winning the bronze, her first medal in international competition.

She barely had time to rest before she was off to yet another competition. A team competition, the Nations Cup, was being held in Germany. When another American skater dropped out at the last minute, Tara was tapped to replace her.

Despite being exhausted, Tara skated well, and three of the seven judges had her ranked first. But the other four selected Irina Slutskaya of Russia. Tara finished second.

That was a victory in itself. Slutskaya was ranked as the third best female skater in the world and had to skate her best in order to defeat Tara.

Tara Lipinski was getting better, and fast.

Chapter Nine:
1996–1997

National Champion

Tara's second-place finish at the Nations Cup shocked the skating world, not to mention Coach Callaghan. He began to realize that Tara was really special. She soaked up his advice like a sponge and was improving rapidly. Perhaps, he thought, it was time to step up the pace and see just how much she could do.

Just two weeks before her final competition of the year, an invitational team exhibition in Philadelphia called the United States Postal Challenge, Callaghan quietly suggested that Tara drop her now familiar triple salchow–triple loop combination in the free skate. Instead, he wanted her to try a triple loop–triple loop, a more difficult move that would earn her higher scores.

Tara couldn't believe her ears. The triple loop–triple loop combo had never been successfully performed in competition.

But Tara liked challenges. The first time she tried the new combination, she nailed it!

But Tara knew it wouldn't be that easy. The next few times she tried the combo, she fell badly.

That didn't stop Tara. Over the new two weeks, she diligently put the two jumps together and eventually got the combo down pat. Yet she still had to integrate it into her program.

It's one thing to complete an element in practice while focusing on nothing else, but it's an entirely different proposition to do so in the middle of an exhausting program. For although figure skating may look easy, it's actually as physically demanding as running as fast as you can for three or four minutes. By the middle of a program, even easy jumps become difficult.

At the Postal Challenge, Tara participated on a team that included Michelle Kwan and Dorothy Hamill, against another team that included her friend Todd Eldredge, Tonia Kwiatkowski, and former national champion Rosalyn Summers. Amid all those skaters, hardly anyone paid any attention to Tara.

Then she skated. And in the midst of her program, it was time to try the triple loop–triple loop.

As she glided backward across the ice, she gathered herself and took a few quick breaths. She had done the combo so many times that by now it seemed like second nature. But she still had to concentrate. Just before she leaped, she visualized herself completing the move perfectly.

Then she jumped, spun through the air three times, and touched down onto the ice. As soon as she did, she was back in the air. Then just as suddenly, she touched down again and was skating on to her next element.

For a second, the arena was silent, then the crowd broke into a roar as they realized what Tara had just accomplished. She was the first skater, male or female, to successfully complete the triple loop–triple loop combination in a public competition. Even though it was just an exhibition, no one could deny that Tara had done what no one else could.

Her teammates shouted with delight and cheered her on. Tara just beamed. Her smile lit up the entire arena.

In competition with some of the biggest stars in skating, both past and present, Tara had stolen the show! And in doing so, she had sent a message to the world that Tara Lipinski was one of the best skaters on the planet.

After the event, the press crowded around her. "How long have you been practicing that move?" someone asked.

"Two weeks," Tara replied. No one could believe it.

Her accomplishment sent shock waves through the skating world. Everyone turned their attention to the 1997 Nationals. Before the Postal Challenge, Michelle Kwan had been everyone's favorite to repeat as the gold medalist. She had won fourteen of the last fifteen competitions in which she had skated. Only Nicole Bobek and Tonia Kwiatkowski had been given any chance of dethroning her.

But Tara's remarkable breakthrough changed everything. All of a sudden, the pressure was on the other skaters. With the triple loop–triple loop combination, Tara's program was more technically difficult and had the potential to earn her higher scores. In order to keep up, the other skaters would have to make changes in their programs, to make them more technically difficult. That's the last thing they wanted to do just before a competition.

The 1997 Nationals were held in Nashville, Tennessee, in mid-February. More than fourteen thousand fans packed the arena for the competition, which was broadcast to a national television audience.

Before the start of the short program, most of the skaters took to the ice to warm up. Tara skated on one end, and Michelle Kwan skated on the other.

Tara was nervous, but she didn't show it. She seemed to skate effortlessly and smiled broadly after completing each element.

Michelle, on the other hand, had the jitters. She was feeling the pressure and fell several times.

She skated her short program before Tara. She fell on her opening jump, a double lutz, and barely hung on through several others.

Still, the judges gave the defending champion the benefit of the doubt. Although her technical scores were below par, she received all 5.8's and 5.9's for presentation, good enough to move her into first place.

Tara hadn't watched Michelle perform and didn't know that she had fallen. She had learned her lesson about watching the competition.

Just before Tara went on, her coach whispered to her, "Just do your thing." Tara nodded and, with a look of determination on her face, took to the ice.

She looked beautiful in a green velvet dress trimmed in lace, an outfit that made her look like a princess and was neither too girlish nor too mature. She looked exactly like a fourteen-year-old, still caught somewhere between childhood and adulthood.

When the music began, she skated confidently. Then she tried her first jump, a triple loop. As fourteen thousand pairs of eyes watched, Tara nailed the jump.

As soon as she landed, a big grin lit up her face. Her confidence grew with each stride, and she tore through her program, doing every required element perfectly. At the end of the program, she was in first place, ahead of the defending world champion!

The free skate was scheduled to take place the following day. That evening, Tara's accomplishment began to sink in. She started getting really nervous.

The next day, as she prepared for the free skate, she told her coach, "I'm not good enough to win. I don't belong here."

Callaghan just smiled at her. "It's okay," he told her. "You're supposed to be nervous. It's okay to feel that way."

Reassured, Tara started to relax. As she warmed up, her confidence grew.

Once again, Michelle Kwan skated before Lipinski. Like Tara, she too was nervous. Except Michelle seemed unable to control her emotions.

After a good start, she attempted a triple lutz–double toe combination, followed closely by a triple lutz–triple toe. Each jump was difficult enough to do alone. To do them back-to-back was doubly hard.

She completed the first combination perfectly but spun out of control on the second. She fell awkwardly onto the ice.

She scrambled to her feet and tried to regain her composure, but it was too late. She almost fell once more, touching her hand to the ice for an automatic deduction, then fell for a second time on a triple lutz. She was so out of sync that she even cut down a later triple to a double. She left the ice in tears.

When her scores were announced, she was still in first place, but there was plenty of room for another skater to overcome her.

A few minutes later, with Michelle still clinging to her lead, it was Tara's turn. Callaghan offered her a few words of encouragement.

"Don't try to win," he cautioned. "Just do your work."

When Tara strode to the center of the rink to begin her program, the crowd responded with chants of "Tara, Tara!" They sensed that something big was about to happen. When Tara heard them, she couldn't help but smile as all the tension melted away. On the ice, it sometimes seemed as if she never stopped smiling.

The music began. Tara started off cleanly, successfully completing each move she attempted. But she knew that the hard stuff was yet to come. The entire program was built around one combination midway through.

Tara and Callaghan had inserted the triple loop–triple loop into her program. It was risky, but they felt it was worth it. If she fell, she'd have no chance of winning. But if she completed the combination and skated cleanly afterward, there would be no way for her to lose.

She gathered herself and launched into the air, reminding herself that it was just like practice.

As she spun through the air, landed briefly, then jumped and spun again, the arena was deathly still.

Then she landed. She had done it! Tara had become the first skater to successfully complete the triple loop–triple loop in competition!

The audience jumped to its feet and started cheering. Tara rode the sound of the crowd's applause throughout the rest of her program, her signature smile filling her face.

When the program ended, the spectators roared some more as Tara took her bows. The chant of "Six! Six! Six!" filled the arena as the audience exhorted the judges to give Tara a perfect score.

Tara skated to the kiss-and-cry area and met her coach. "I'm so proud of you," Callaghan said as he gave her a hug.

But Tara was still nervous as she waited for her scores. She knew that she had skated well, but she worried that the judges still might not give her high marks for her presentation.

She needn't have worried. As the scores flashed onto the scoreboard, the crowd let loose with a resounding roar. Every mark was either a 5.8 or a 5.9. All Tara could say was "Oh, my God!"

Tara Lipinski was the United States Ladies Singles Skating Champion.

She liked the way that sounded.

Chapter Ten:
1997

World Champion

Tara had little time to enjoy her triumph. The 1997 World Championships were only a month away. Michelle Kwan and Nicole Bobek, who had finished second and third at the Nationals, would be competing along with Tara.

But now there were distractions everywhere. Tara's win was big news, and her history-making triple loop–triple loop was shown over and over on the news. All of a sudden, everyone wanted to meet Tara.

The next few days were a whirlwind as she made a number of television appearances, including one on one of her favorite shows, *Late Night with David Letterman.*

But Pat Lipinski and Coach Callaghan made sure that Tara stayed focused. Soon she was back on the ice. She had another competition, the Champions Series Finals, to skate before going to the Worlds. It was a tough event that matched the best skaters from the United States, Russia, Canada, Japan, and several other countries. Michelle Kwan would have a chance to regain her confidence. Tara wanted to prove that her win was no fluke.

Michelle was determined to win. Although she and Tara were friendly off the ice, on the ice they were arch rivals. "This is a fight," declared Kwan, trying to motivate herself. "This is war."

Tara was more relaxed. "I just want to do my best," she said.

The competition was a repeat of the Nationals. When Michelle stumbled and fell, Tara took advantage of the opportunity and skated well, narrowly winning the competition and a fifty-thousand-dollar prize.

Over the next few weeks, Tara continued training for the Worlds. She tried to stay focused. Everything was happening so fast, she could hardly believe it.

She left for the Worlds, held in Lausanne, Switzerland, in March 1997, full of anticipation and anxiety. She was excited about competing, but she was also concerned.

Her appearance in the competition was controversial. A new rule stated that every skater had to be at least fifteen years old in order to compete.

Although Tara was only fourteen, she had been allowed in because she had competed in the event previously. But some members of the skating community still didn't believe she belonged. Just after she arrived, she learned that if she won, she would become the youngest world champion ever, even younger than the great Sonja Henie, who had been just a few months older than Tara when she had won her first World Championship. Everyone was watching Tara closely to see if she could take the pressure.

The European press was particularly interested in Tara. So many journalists attended her first press conference that Tara, who was only four-foot-eight, had to stand on a chair so they could see her while she answered questions!

They tried to stir up a controversy by creating a rivalry between Tara and Michelle Kwan, but neither girl would have anything to do with it. "She's not my rival," said Tara diplomatically. "She's my idol."

Tara stayed calm and made it through the qualifier easily. It helped calm her nerves and build her confidence.

The men's competition was held first. Tara enjoyed watching her friend Todd compete. But as the women's competition approached, she began to get nervous again.

Then, the day before the short program, the American skaters were stunned to learn that Carlo Fassi, Nicole Bobek's coach, had died of a heart attack. He was a close friend of Richard Callaghan. Tara knew her coach was upset. She was determined to give him something to smile about.

He had tried to keep the pressure off her all week by telling the press, "I don't think she's going to win it [the gold medal], and neither does she." That may have been true, but both Tara and her coach knew she wanted to win.

Her coach had been there for her, and now it was Tara's turn to do something for him.

Tara took to the ice for the short program in her green velvet dress. Callaghan again gave her his usual advice. "Don't try to win," he admonished. "Just do your work. You're ready for this."

Tara stood like a ballerina as the music began to play. Then she began skating. She quickly built up speed and launched into a triple lutz, a difficult jump to make anytime, not to mention as the opening move of a program, when a skater is just becoming accustomed to the ice.

She landed perfectly and positioned herself for the next element, which she also performed perfectly. With each additional element, her confidence rose. By the end of the program, she was flying through the air, skating as well as she ever had in her life.

Former champion Peggy Fleming, serving as a commentator on American television, summed up the feelings of all those in attendance. "Wow!" was all she could say.

Apart from one 5.5, all Tara's marks were 5.8.

One year before, she had stumbled and fallen to twenty-third place. Now she was in first.

But Michelle Kwan still had to skate, as well as several other young women. Tara could only wait and see if her score would hold up.

Michelle was determined to prove she was out of her slump, and she stepped onto the ice with determination etched on her face. She skated a beautiful program but stumbled on the landing of one jump, a critical mistake that cost her a few valuable points.

Her marks were good, but not good enough to finish in the top three. She was fourth at the end of the short program, still in the hunt for the title. Tara remained in first place.

"I'm satisfied," she told the press later. "This gives me a lot of confidence." She was particularly pleased by the reception of the judges. They weren't looking at her like a little girl anymore. They saw her as a skater.

The next day was the free skate. When Tara took to the ice, the championship was hers to win. This time, she wore an elegant white dress with gold trim. She looked like something out of a fairy tale.

Perhaps because of her age, Tara seems to have the ability to appear as if she is making up her program as she goes along. She never looks like she's bored or tired or doing something that she's already done hundreds of times before. She exudes enthusiasm.

When she heard the music begin, the butterflies in her stomach flew off. With a serious smile on her face, she launched into her program.

She first landed a perfect triple flip before attempting a triple lutz–double toe combination. In the air she was perfect, but she landed hard.

That didn't faze Tara. She dug the toothed edge of her skate into the ice and hung on.

Her confidence was at a peak. She soared into the second half of her program and pulled off a dramatic triple loop–triple lutz, another combination no one had ever landed in competition before.

As the crowd began to cheer, Tara's pleasure shone on her face. As she spun to a conclusion, everyone in the arena stood and applauded.

By the time Tara reached the kiss-and-cry area, she was in tears, but they were tears of joy. Coach Callaghan held her by her shoulders, smiled, and yelled, "Awesome!" She knew she had put herself in a position to win.

That feeling was confirmed when her scores were posted. Every judge had given her either a 5.8 or a 5.9. Tara was in first place!

Now she had to wait and watch while other

skaters tried to catch her. It came down to Michelle Kwan.

As Michelle took to the ice, her coach, Frank Carroll, gave her a strong piece of advice: "Attack; don't defend." Like many observers, he thought her recent slump stemmed from trying to be too careful and too perfect. To have any chance of winning, she had to let go and just skate. "I just let myself fly," she said later.

Kwan silenced her critics with a spectacular, almost perfect performance. No matter how well she skated, Tara could not yet match the older skater's elegance and sophistication. Kwan, too, left the ice to a standing ovation.

All eyes were focused on the judges. Both Tara and Michelle had given performances worthy of a world champion. But only one of them could win the gold medal.

Tara waited backstage as the scores were announced. By the narrowest of margins, Michelle Kwan had won the free skate program.

But that wasn't enough to win the world championship. When the performance in the short program and the free skate were added together, Tara Lipinski's name was on top!

For the first time in her skating career, Tara seemed overwhelmed. "I never expected it," she said, stunned. Then, as she stood on the podium with a gold medal around her neck, "The Star-Spangled Banner" playing over the loudspeakers, she could barely contain her emotions. Up in the stands, her parents cried.

Tara Lipinski was the best skater in the world.

Chapter Eleven:
1997-1998

Life at the Top

In the wake of her upset victory, Tara's life changed dramatically, both on and off the ice.

She was now more famous than she could ever have imagined. Whenever she appeared in public, people asked her for her autograph. She was constantly being asked to make television appearances or give interviews. Although she enjoyed her celebrity status, it also brought some unwelcome attention.

People she had never met placed expectations on her behavior. "I think they expect me to be like a nineteen-year-old," she told one reporter. "No matter how hard I try, I'm only fourteen."

Despite all her hard work and how many times she told everyone that she loved to skate, some tried to use her as a symbol for children who had been pushed too hard by their parents. Others viewed her as a spoiled brat.

She soon returned to the ice, the one place where she felt most comfortable. In the spring of 1997, she went on a six-city tour with the World Figure Skating Champions before returning to Detroit to prepare new programs for the upcoming skating season. Her unexpected win had suddenly made the 1998 Olympics the focus of her attention.

Tara and Coach Callaghan selected new music and new costumes and worked with Tara's choreographer to create brand-new short and long programs. It was important to change every year because, as Tara grew older, she was becoming a different skater. Her body was beginning to develop, and she was growing taller and heavier.

The season would begin with several invitational competitions in the fall. Then the Nationals would be held in Philadelphia in January 1998, followed closely by the Winter Olympics, in Nagano, Japan, in February. The Nationals were usually expected to provide a preview of the Olympics. The American national champion would become the odds-on favorite to win the gold medal in Nagano. And many experts believed that the American skaters had a good chance to win all three medals.

Tara's first big competition was Skate America, held in October 1997. Although Tara skated well, Michelle Kwan came back to resume her dominance of ladies singles competition, beating Tara convincingly.

A month later, at the Trophée Lalique competition in France, Tara tried to get on track. Michelle skipped the event, making Tara a heavy favorite.

Tara skated a flawless short program to lead the competition. It appeared as if she was ready to take her place on the victory podium.

But in the free skate, she did poorly. She appeared to struggle from the moment she took the ice. Skating tentatively, she turned two triple jumps into doubles and gave a lackluster performance that impressed neither the judges nor the crowd. Most of her scores ranged from 5.5 to 5.8, but one judge gave her a mediocre technical score of 5.3. She finished second to French skater Laetitia Hubert.

Tara had a good reason for her below-par performance. She had a bad cold, and the night before the free skate, she had had trouble sleeping. But she refused to make excuses. "Once you are world champion, there is a little more pressure," she said. "I think I just tried a little too hard."

Over the next two months, Tara tried to get back on track. There were whispers in the skating community that success had come too early for her and that she wasn't mentally prepared to defend her title as world champion. Some speculated that she was burned out from competing, while others said that as she grew, she simply wasn't able to skate as well as she had when she was younger and smaller.

Meanwhile, Michelle Kwan, who had had to stop training for a few weeks due to a stress fracture in one of her toes, had resumed training and was skating beautifully. Nicole Bobek had recovered from a series of disappointing performances the year before and was also skating well. Kwan, Bobek, and Lipinski would be competing next at the 1998 National Championships.

Tara's troubles continued at that important event. In her short program, she fell on her triple flip, a jump she usually completed with ease. The error caused her to finish the short program in fourth place.

Kwan easily won the short program by recording a magnificent seven perfect marks of 6.0 for presentation, while Bobek and Tonia Kwiatkowski finished second and third.

Tara's performance even put her Olympic dreams at risk. Although she could still be selected for the team even if she didn't medal, if she stumbled badly in the free skate and the three skaters ahead of her all did well, the U.S. skating team officials could conceivably leave her off the team. When Tara took to the ice for her free skate, she was determined to make it to Nagano.

She knew it was almost impossible for her to repeat as national champion. Even if she placed first in the long program, Kwan would have to finish third or lower for Lipinski to retain her title, and both Bobek and Kwiatkowski would have to skate poorly as well.

With nothing to lose, Tara and Coach Callaghan had gone all out planning her free skate, scheduling an amazing eight triples.

She skated well, but Michelle Kwan was magnificent once more. Still, Tara finished in second place, winning the silver medal, while Bobek won the bronze. Tara was disappointed not to have defended her title but relieved to know that she was still going to Japan. She had heard her parents tell the story about the time she had watched the Olympic medal ceremony, then stood on the plastic box and asked her mother for flowers and a ribbon.

Now she had a chance to do that for real.

Chapter Twelve:
1998

The Olympic Experience

Before the Olympic Games, Tara's parents and Coaches Callaghan and Faulkner decided that it would be best for Tara if she stayed in the United States during the games and traveled to Japan only a few days before her competition, scheduled to take place near the end of the games. That's what Michelle Kwan and Nicole Bobek were planning to do.

And even when Tara arrived in Japan, they wanted her to stay in a hotel far away from the distractions of the Olympic village, where most athletes stay for the duration of the Olympics.

Tara was crestfallen. She had dreamed about going to the Olympics for her entire life. To her, the Olympics meant far more than the few short minutes she would spend on the ice competing.

Tara believed in the Olympic ideal, which empha-sizes sportsmanship and understanding among peo-ple from different cultures. When she had dreamed about the Olympics, that's what she had thought about, not just winning a medal. She wanted to be a part of the whole experience. Her teammates at the Detroit Skating Club, including Todd Eldredge, had told her all about previous Olympics, about how much fun they had staying in the village and meet-ing athletes from around the world.

When her parents and Richard Callaghan told her of their decision, Tara spoke up. She wanted to go to the opening ceremonies, and she wanted to stay in the Olympic village. "Even if I don't win a medal," she pleaded, "I'll always have the Olympics." Al-though they didn't agree with her, her parents and her coach knew that they didn't have the right to deny Tara a complete Olympic experience. They grudgingly gave in, although they still wanted Tara to leave Nagano a few days before the competition to train in private.

Tara arrived at the Olympic village before the games began and checked in with the rest of the American team. She stayed in the barracks-like dormitory, rooming with another skater. She took full advantage of all the Olympics had to offer. She ate in the large cafeteria with the other athletes, spent hours in the video game room, and stayed up late talking with athletes from all over the world.

She loved it. Every moment was just as she had imagined, only better. But at the same time, she didn't forget about her competition.

She couldn't wait to start practicing. She was thrilled to step onto the ice at the White Ring, the Olympic skating facility, for her first practice session.

Despite all the excitement of the previous few days, Tara's first practice session went perfectly, as she nailed every element she tried and skated as well as she ever had in her life.

When she left the ice after her first practice, she had an experience that illustrated why she had wanted to stay in Nagano.

Although the practice session was supposed to be closed to the public, Akebono, the sumo wrestling grand champion of Japan, had heard about Tara and wanted to meet her. Sumo wrestlers are huge, and sumo wrestling is one of the most popular sports in Japan. Akebono, who weighs over four hundred pounds, could go anywhere he wanted!

As Tara left the ice, Akebono came down to meet her. Tara looked at him in wide-eyed wonder. She had never seen anyone so big. He was at least five times bigger than she was! When he reached out to her, Tara watched in amazement as his gigantic hand seemed to swallow hers. He wished her good luck and left. When he was gone, Tara burst out laughing.

Experiences like that convinced Tara's parents and her coaches that Tara had been right about the Olympics. After only a few days, they saw how much she was enjoying herself, how relaxed she appeared to be, and how well she was skating. They agreed to let her stay in Nagano for the entire Olympics. Pat Lipinski later admitted that allowing Tara to stay in the village was "the smartest thing we ever did."

For the next ten days, as she continued her training, Tara was a familiar sight in Nagano. She made friends with several members of the United States gold medal–winning ice hockey team, and they teased each other about skating. Other famous Olympic athletes went out of their way to meet her, and Tara traded Olympic team pins with the other athletes in the village, an Olympic tradition. She also spent time in the sewing room, gossiping with other athletes and making a pillow to take back home. As far as Tara was concerned, being at the Olympics was even better than going to Disney World, a place she had visited nearly a dozen times.

But as the time for the skating competition neared, Tara cut back on her social life and focused on her skating. Entering the competition, she was confident and skating well. So far, her Olympic experience had matched her dreams.

But few observers gave her much of a chance to win. Former men's champion Scott Hamilton, who covered the event for American television, was one of the few people who gave Tara a shot at the gold medal. "She's the best technical skater in the world," he pointed out, "and her long program is the most difficult of anyone in the competition. If she skates clean, she could win." But even he admitted that if Michelle Kwan skated cleanly as well, the gold medal was all but hers.

The ladies singles competition began on Wednesday, February 18. That evening, American television spent most of their air time focused on Michelle, who had finally arrived in Nagano. Tara had been a good story, but now Kwan got all the attention. That was fine with Tara.

As the skaters warmed up before the event, both Michelle and Tara looked nervous. Each girl fell while attempting a jump.

Tara skated before her rival. Although it is usually a disadvantage to skate first, for Tara, it was probably for the best. She didn't worry about skating better than Michelle. She focused only on skating as well as she could.

After warming up for a few moments, she skated to the edge of the ice and spoke briefly with Callaghan. Then she strode confidently out to the center of the rink and stood motionless as she waited for the music to start.

For her short program, she and Callaghan had selected music from *Anastasia,* the animated Disney film about the young Russian princess. It was appropriate for Tara, who at age fifteen, was still a huge fan of Disney films. Her dress, a sparkling, beaded white-and-blue outfit, echoed the film. It looked like something a princess would wear.

As the music started, Tara pushed off and began her program. She started slowly, matching the music. She looked beautiful as she gracefully gained speed, then went into a spiral sequence.

When she spun out of the sequence, she gained speed with the music and prepared for her first jump, a triple lutz–double loop combination. In recent months, the combination had given her trouble. She was supposed to take off from the back outside edge of her skate. But once in a while, she made a tiny mistake and left from the back inside edge. It was a small mistake, but one she knew the judges would be looking for.

Quickly skating backward, she gathered her momentum, dug her toe into the ice, and vaulted into the air. To most observers, her takeoff looked perfect.

Spinning three times in the air, she landed as required on her opposite foot and immediately launched into the air again for the double loop. She spun and landed smoothly.

Her face showed what she thought of her effort. Her smile said it all.

As the pace of the music increased, so did the

pace of Tara's skating. Moving her arms expertly to the music, she now focused on her next jump, a triple flip, the same one she had missed at the Nationals.

This time she didn't miss. She was perfect.

As she glided out of her landing, she thrust her arms out toward the crowd as if she was about to give everyone a hug. Her smile grew larger.

Brimming with confidence, she surged on. The next required element was a double axel, for which she had to spin two and half times in the air.

She nailed it and seemed to float through the remainder of her program as if her skates were hardly touching the ice. Then as the music reached a crescendo, she settled into her final maneuver, a combination spin.

Although spins are easy for most skaters, in competition they must be executed precisely. A skater is supposed to stay in place. If she drifts during the spin, she can lose points.

Tara spun as if anchored to the ice, ending with her arms thrust toward the sky as the music ended.

As the audience burst into applause, Tara smiled some more. Tears filled her eyes, and she put her hands to her head in joy. Then, as some members of the crowd chanted, "U.S.A.! U.S.A.!" she half-ran and half-skated off the ice to Coach Callaghan and Coach Faulkner.

"Awesome!" yelled Callaghan over the tumult. "Awesome! That was big time!"

"Beautiful!" echoed Faulkner.

Tara then looked at the television camera focused on her. "Hi, Daddy," she cried. "Hi, Mom." For although her parents were in Nagano, they had been too nervous to sit in the crowd. They had watched her skate on television.

As Tara sat between her coaches in the kiss-and-cry area, she added greetings to her friends back home in the United States and blew them a kiss.

"That was so cool," she blurted out.

Everyone was tense as they waited for her scores to be posted.

The technical marks came first. They were all 5.6's to 5.8's. Very, very good, but not great. A few judges had thought she began her triple lutz–double loop on the wrong edge.

To remain in contention for a gold medal, Tara needed to score better for her presentation. That had long been a problem. But she had worked incredibly hard on precisely that part of her program. She hoped the judges had been paying attention and had judged her based on what they saw on the ice, rather than on any preconceived notion of what a fifteen-year-old skater could do.

When her marks flashed on the scoreboard, Callaghan immediately shouted, "Yes!" and nearly leaped into the air. Her scores ranged from 5.6 to 5.9. That put her in first place. But Michelle Kwan still had to skate.

Tara was delighted with her performance. "This is the first time at the end of my program that I wanted to cry," she said later. "I felt it was one of my best programs ever. Everything just came together. I didn't want to get off the ice tonight."

Callaghan agreed. "She did her best skating of the year," he said. "That was the best artistry she has ever done."

Tara then did something few other skaters did. After performing, most leave the rink or remain backstage.

But after changing from her outfit, she went out into the arena and found her friends in the crowd, taking a seat on someone's lap because there weren't any empty seats. Her night as a skater was over, so now she became a spectator like everyone else. This was the Olympics, after all, and she wanted to see the rest of the competition.

So she sat watching as Michelle Kwan took to the ice for her short program. While Tara's marks were good, Kwan skated knowing that there was still plenty of room for her to overtake Tara.

As Tara looked on, Kwan skated a clean program, although it lacked the energy of her stellar achievement at the Nationals. Although her technical scores were almost identical to Tara's, she received higher marks for her presentation. At the end of the short program, eight of the nine judges had Michelle in first place. One judge ranked Tara first, and the others had her in second place.

Still, Tara was pleased. She had skated well, and she wasn't finished yet. The long program would be worth two-thirds of her score.

Besides, this was the Olympics! Tara was having the time of her life.

Chapter Thir...
1998

A Golden Moment

With the free skate scheduled for Friday, February 20, Tara had a day to catch her breath and prepare for the most important skating performance of her life. She even agreed to leave the Olympic village and stay in a hotel with her parents Thursday night. She knew she had to have a good night's sleep. The Olympics were almost over, and life in the village was becoming a little rowdy, as most competitors were celebrating and starting to unwind.

Although Tara didn't forget where she was, she tried not to let herself be overwhelmed with thoughts of the upcoming competition. Before she left the hotel for the rink on Friday afternoon, she ate a big plate of spaghetti, then told her mother she wanted to talk. "I'm scared," she said.

Pat Lipinski nodded and told her, "You have a

to be scared. But you're going to do it. You have to believe that."

Then Tara gave her mother a big kiss, looked her in the eye, and said, "I'm going to do it." She left for the rink, then returned and knocked on the door of her mother's room a moment later. When her mother opened the door, Tara smiled and said, "Happy birthday, Mom." Pat broke into a smile. With love in her eyes, she watched her daughter bounce away as if she didn't have a care in the world.

When the competition began, the White Ring was packed to capacity, and millions of people around the world sat glued to their television sets.

Tara got lucky in the draw. Michelle would skate before she did. She hoped the judges would leave room for the possibility that she would skate better.

Kwan looked nervous before taking to the ice. She knew she had a big lead and didn't want to make any mistakes. Tara remained backstage, concerned only with her own performance. She knew that if she paid attention to Michelle, she might lose her focus.

Michelle proceeded to skate a clean program without any mistake that appeared as if it might cost her the gold medal. The only flaw was a slight misstep in her landing after a triple flip, and her pace. She had skated cautiously. The performance had been technically sound, but it had been curiously unexciting and passionless, as if she were somehow emotionally detached. Although she received all 5.9's for her presentation, she received five 5.7's and four 5.8's for her technical marks. She left the ice in tears, partially with joy for having completed her program in position to win, partially with relief for finally achieving her goal of skating in the Olympics, and partially with concern over whether she had skated well enough to hold off Tara.

Twenty minutes later, it was Tara's turn to skate. Although she didn't know Michelle's exact score, she knew that Kwan had skated well but left the door open for her. Tara was determined to skate right through that narrow opening, just as she had been able to squeeze between older and more experienced skaters while playing roller hockey years before. If she had learned anything in her young life, she knew it was a mistake to underestimate what she could accomplish.

Wearing an elegant royal blue dress, and a determined look, she warmed up in the almost silent arena. The more she skated, the more comfortable she appeared.

Then she strode over to where Callaghan and Faulkner stood, next to the kiss-and-cry area. The two whispered words of encouragement.

When the announcer called her name, Tara's face lit up and she skated to the center of the ice to begin her program. Over the next four and a half minutes, she would have the opportunity to complete the dream that had begun so long ago when she had asked her mother for a ribbon and some flowers. Years of preparation were coming down to just a few short minutes.

Tara stood absolutely still as she waited for her music — a selection from *The Rainbow* — to begin. As she recalled later, she had a sudden revelation when she began her program. "I knew what the Olympics were all about — pure joy — and I put that into my program." In what should have been the most nerve-racking moment of her life, Tara Lipinski was happier than she could ever recall being.

The music started slowly. Tara skated in step to the melody, performing a perfect spin sequence before launching into an equally perfect double axel.

She tried to hear the music and allow herself to move within it.

As the music brightened, Tara launched into her first triple, the flip. She soared upward, spun, then landed as delicately as a leaf landing on water. She broke out into a relaxed grin and increased her pace.

She then took off into a triple lutz–double toe. This time, there was no doubt — her takeoff had been perfect. When she landed cleanly, Callaghan called out to her, "That's gorgeous!"

As she completed each element, her confidence soared and she seemed increasingly inspired. She flew out of a second spin sequence, looking as if she were skating just for the fun of it. She might as well have been all alone on a frozen pond in the middle of the woods.

As the music changed to a selection entitled *Scenes of Summer,* Tara's skating style subtly evolved to match it. Only a few feet from where the judges sat watching, she skated into her triple loop–triple loop combination.

Again, it was perfect. As she landed, she spread her arms wide and gave a gigantic smile, then effort-lessly sent herself across the ice and into a triple lutz. The crowd began to sense that she had a chance to win. On television, commentator Scott Hamilton started calling out each of her elements in an ever more excited voice.

After another triple lutz, Tara prepared for the final jump of her program. It wasn't just a combination of two jumps but a combination of three, a triple toe–half loop–triple salchow.

It was a bold, difficult maneuver, one few other skaters would dare even try, made doubly hard by the fact that it was coming nearly four minutes into the program. At that point most skaters are so exhausted they wouldn't think to try any kind of combination, much less one with three jumps.

But Tara and her coaches had put the jump at this point in the program for a reason. It was so daring and difficult that if she nailed it, it was certain to impress the judges.

By this time, Tara was skating so effortlessly that she didn't feel any fatigue. She took to the air in a blur, spinning then landing and spinning again, then landing and spinning in the air once more in a single uninterrupted motion.

When she landed, she nearly burst with happiness, and the crowd cheered enthusiastically, as if they, too, were taking part in her performance. She sailed into her final spin, then stopped in time with the music as the applause of the crowd took over.

Tara thrust her arms into the air over her head like a boxer after a knockout, then ran off the ice toward her coaches.

Richard Callaghan pounded his hands on the boards and cried, "Yes! Yes! Yes!" Tara burst into tears and held her hands to her head as if in utter disbelief.

"I'm so proud of you," said Callaghan as Tara sobbed, speechless. "I've never seen anybody handle pressure like that," he added. "You were awesome!" Tara hugged both her coaches before sitting between them in the kiss-and-cry area, her feet barely touching the floor. Then, remembering an aunt who was in the hospital, she looked to the camera and said, "Hi, Aunt Mary. Hi, Daddy."

As someone handed her a huge bouquet of flowers, she looked out at the world and said, "That was so cool. I can't believe it, it was so good." Then she turned to Megan Faulkner and gave her another huge hug.

But it was still too early to celebrate. Tara had given the performance of her life, but unless the judges thought so, too, it would only be enough for a silver medal.

Her technical scores flashed on the scoreboard first, and an announcer read them out loud.

Tara squealed. She received three 5.8's and six 5.9's! Callaghan and Faulkner held their breath and waited for the presentation scores. They would know immediately if Tara had won the gold medal, for when the presentation scores are posted, so is the skater's placement in the competition.

The instant they appeared, Tara announced to the world that she was the gold medalist. She screamed with delight and leaped to her feet, jumping up and down and sobbing, "I can't believe it, I can't believe it." She'd received five 5.8's and four 5.9's. Six of the nine judges had put her in first place. Michelle Kwan was the silver medalist, and Lu Chen of China won the bronze.

On television, Scott Hamilton called it "the upset of all upsets."

Immediately following her performance, Tara was at once effusive and humble. She called her father, who was elsewhere in the arena, and wished him a happy birthday. Then she did a brief interview, and told the press, "Like, I'm in shock. I can't believe I'm Olympic champion. Everything was perfect tonight — the lighting, everything. I'll never forget it."

Then it was time for the medal ceremony. Still wearing her beautiful royal blue skating dress, tiny Tara Lipinski led Michelle Kwan and Lu Chen to the three-tiered podium in the center of the rink. The crowd cheered. Then she stepped to the top box, just as she had in her living room fourteen years earlier.

A Japanese girl in a kimono solemnly walked to center ice, bearing a bouquet of flowers and a gold medal attached to a loop of ribbon. An Olympic official took the flowers and handed them to Tara. Then he picked up the gold medal and turned to face her.

Tara bowed her head slightly, and the man hung the medal around her neck.

As the ceremony was repeated for Kwan and Chen, Tara held the precious medal with both hands, looking at it over and over again as if the entire moment were part of some fabulous dream she could hardly believe.

Then all three young women turned and watched as three large flags, two American and one Chinese, were hoisted into the air. As the first notes of "The Star-Spangled Banner" began to drift through the arena, Tara placed her hand on her heart and tried hard to stand tall and proud. But she couldn't resist the urge to glance down at her medal once more.

A tired smile on her face, she closed her eyes for a moment and tried to feel everything all at once. Her Olympic experience was complete. Her dream was fulfilled.

Tara didn't go to bed until four A.M. She fell asleep with her gold medal still around her neck. When she awoke, it was the first thing she looked for.

It was still there. Her dream *had* come true.

"Look," she told an interviewer later that morning as she traced the medal with her fingers. "It's the rising sun and the mountains in the back. It's so cool."

Matt Christopher

Sports Bio Bookshelf

Andre Agassi

John Elway

Wayne Gretzky

Ken Griffey Jr.

Mia Hamm

Grant Hill

Randy Johnson

Michael Jordan

Lisa Leslie

Tara Lipinski

Greg Maddux

Hakeem Olajuwon

Emmitt Smith

Mo Vaughn

Tiger Woods

Steve Young

The #1 Sports Writer for Kids

MATT CHRISTOPHER

Read them all!

Mountain Bike Mania

No Arm in Left Field

Olympic Dream

Penalty Shot

Pressure Play

Prime-Time Pitcher

Red-Hot Hightops

The Reluctant Pitcher

Return of the Home Run Kid

Roller Hockey Radicals

Run, Billy, Run

Shoot for the Hoop

Shortstop from Tokyo

Skateboard Tough

Snowboard Maverick

Soccer Halfback

Soccer Scoop

Spike It!

The Submarine Pitch

Supercharged Infield

Tackle Without a Team

Takedown

The Team That Couldn't Lose

Tight End

Too Hot to Handle

Top Wing

Touchdown for Tommy

Tough to Tackle

Undercover Tailback

Wingman on Ice

The Winning Stroke

The Year Mom Won the Pennant

All available in paperback from Little, Brown and Company